PIT STOPS and PROTON BEAMS

Aurelio Rico Lopez III

Copyright © Aurelio Rico Lopez III
Copyright © Hybrid Sequence Media
Cover Design © Malgorzata Mika

All rights reserved. No part of this publication may be reproduced, distributed, or transmitted in any form or by any means, including photocopying, recording, or other electronic or mechanical methods, without prior written permission of the publisher. Permitted by copyright law.

This is a work of fiction. Names, characters, businesses, places, events, and incidents are either the products of the author's imagination or used in a fictitious manner. Any resemblance to actual persons, living or dead, or actual events is purely coincidental.

ISBN: 979-8-9878449-2-2

Hybrid Sequence Media
Massachusetts, US

hybridsequencemedia.wordpress.com

Massachusetts - Philippines

Advance Praise

"A minimalist approach to and extrapolation from SF tropes with more than two hundred haiku. Clever, entertaining, at times incisive and at times laugh-out-loud."
-Bruce Boston, author of *Spacers Snarled int he Hair of Comets*.

"The haiku becomes a singularity alien that mutates, lives in your heart, and never dies in this awesome exploration of syllables, space and soul."
-Christoph Paul, author of Horror Film Poems

"Sci-Fi fun!
Whimsical, different and a brilliant reversal of the haiku.
In your best Alien voice, I highly recommend to read this collection again and again.
Such a humorous Gem!
-Sharon Ferrante, author of The Choir of Crickets

For my mother
Merna G. Rico Lopez
who got me hooked on reading
and writing,
among other things.

PIT STOPS and PROTON BEAMS

> If you think this Universe is bad,
> you should see some of the others.
> -Philip K. Dick

great Venusian war
skies rain ash
snowflakes in December

alien mother
closes cryo-chamber door
pleasant dreams, child

surreal encounter
alien flags down trucker
to borrow cellphone

empty desert road
spacecraft barrels out of control
male coyote yawns

NASA launched time capsule
of goodwill
smashing into warship

Santa flies just north
over restricted air space
surface missiles hum

Area 51
pale-faced soldier fright
the captive is loose

odd warning from space
look out below
meteor shower

it's a late night shift
radar operator snores
armada descends

captain flips launch switch
the engines incinerate
infecting the crew

let's say we just made first contact
astronaut sneezes
inadvertently declares war

extraterrestrial grins
human pops enclosure
such a pathetic weak mind

astronaut signs off
walks off to sleeping chambers
air supply lapse out

craft crashed into barn
apologized to cow
the pilot stumbled

The officer fumes over
alien graffiti
also known as crop circles

discovered research reveals
Martian DNA
is ninety percent human

human-sized insects
bug-eating foliage
can't tell difference

cranium opened
alien medical team
marvel primitive brain

invading horde
armed with sonic pulses
killer beats, man!

alien returns from Earth
rings, gold chains, fur coat
"humans call it swag," it says

Martian summer camp
kids gather 'round campfire
tales of the humans

year 2141
class trip to museum
exhibit nine labelled "Book"

an uncharted planet
team leader coughs
dooms alien species

watchtower sentry
trick of light
yet swears, rocks have moved

shape-shifting race defeated
heroes welcomed home
fingerprints do not pair up

virulent illness
escape pod blasts toward Earth
rash on pilot's neck

rapt council
gather around Earth weapon
Caps Lock key

nocturnal winged beasts
detesting light
last flare sputters out

a crashed space vessel
hiker investigates ship
twig snaps behind him

dimensional portal
time wasted celebrating
door sway and rock both ways

lone asteroid, habitat
to ravenous beasts
drawn by Earth's gravity

alien jungle
last transmission
don't water the plants

hovering in space
astronaut calls for answers
deafening silence

man hammers flag on surface
vibrates dinner bells
for creatures within the sphere

    tracks on ground leading to?
    a two-legged thing—
    "Zork, we are not alone"

        soldier boxed in
        enemy slithers closer
        pulls grenade pin

Travel Advisory:
when visiting Earth
watch out for those billboards

ponder nursery rhyme
cow jumped over moon
bovine superpower

the weekend camping trip
bags all packed
blaster for good measure

Venusian beach
lifeguards with proton cannons
recent shark problem

galaxy's biggest threat
not hulking leviathan
but speck on petri dish

decorated captain
slams fist on console
thing unfazed by rockets

plastic gun holsters
arcade game beyond repair
poor Martian the sore loser

icy cliffs of Neptune
unimpressed tourist
tosses away brochure

alien safari
WARNING to First-Timers:
do not feed the tour guide

bones litter the cavern floor
no sign of predator...
sudden flap of giant wings

picnic goers scream
bug spray not gonna cut it
massive Buick gnats

"alien unscathed by bullets?
impenetrable skin
I knew I should've called in sick"

secret laboratory
doctor in need of shower
post-mortem explosion

robotic infant
it beeps unplugged in protest
from its power source

open mic auditions
creature shrieks in alien tongue
wins a record contract

there's no use hiding
heightened olfactory sense
creatures can smell you

    photo album
    sunrises on Saturn
    cheese steaks at Chuck's

        I'd gladly give up three limbs
        to spawn with you, LOVE
        bizarre alien love letter

unforeseen circumstance
violin string's — strums
music tames savage beast

an elated youngster
trade of a lifetime
baseball card for blaster

motherly advice:
make new friends, she said nothing
about aliens

timely stroke of luck
New Year's fireworks display
scares off invaders

brand new dating app
is a hit, find your soul mate
in your galaxy

endowed with two brains
strange alien visitor
argues with itself

frustrated E.T.
crash landing in the Gobi
sunscreen back at home

Martian workout gym
big muscular aliens
lifting with their minds

battle for survival
a shocking revelation
remotely controlled foe

alien day-care
screams of terror fill the room
Boortean Brood is loose

a roadside diner
they can't even pronounce dish
apologetic cook

intelligent plant-life
leguminous, boards spaceship
peas in a pod... clever!

all hell broke lose
when robot collected rocks
and samples hatched

a bizarre planet
where canines rule, and humans
chow down on homework

duck, weave, dodge, and PUNCH!
interstellar boxing match
watch for that left claw

one week on Earth passed
search for intelligent life
nothing... look elsewhere

alien walks in
gasoline station in the boonies
buys map of Texas

captain's log, Star-Date
who gives a... creatures increase!
fear ship's door won't hold

New Discovery!
heed the pollen of Klaanthean
transudes the spacesuits

landing gear shutdown
Houston, we have a problem
gremlins are onboard

a feral underground race
starving dormant for years
visitors slow and clumsy

ship hovers unseen
pilots study blue planet
thought it'd be bigger?

adopting culture
spray paint in alien's hand
Nortepus Wuz Here !!

abduction control
exasperated Martian
more than enough cows

alien place of worship
astronaut dumbfounded
deity looks like Elvis

grumpy old alien
private property
trespassers will be zapped

a vast sea of space
finned creatures circle shuttle
like sharks drawn by chum

youngster at pet shop
homo sapiens on sale
father points, Half Price!

intoxicated alien
spends night in town jail
under pretense of FUI

victors rewrite history
for shits-n-giggles
primate ancestry code

inside used bookstore
aliens browse sci-fi section
with stifled laughter

a blast from the past
on planet light years away
supernova shines

a galactic restaurant
beaked diner squawks
buffalo wings on menu

that crude propulsion device, SUCKS!
commendable effort
alien returns boy's slingshot

primitive race
worship metallic god
NASA Rover

ameboid entity
propagate by division
a mind-splitting process

asteroid belt encountered
tentacled pilot curses
newly paint job—Ruined!

can anyone hear me?
buzz of static
message falls on, dead ears

zero gravity
this inflatable life craft
Point This Side Up, shown

it's precious cargo
within the rear of ship's hull
first instinct to feed

dinosaurs roam Earth
reset program
meteor shower

this Martian dress shop
has such limited choices
everything in red

erratic flight pattern
student flyer
pilot sweats profusely

soaring at light speed
a collision imminent
mad game of chicken

avid collector
Da Vinci has nothing on
Almighty Xelabff!

shuttle ablaze
no choice but to eject
face what's outside

scattered debris drifts
a space mishap in limbo
helmet bobs — beach ball

horizon sunset
man tosses log in fire
creatures can't bear light

predator watches
the newcomers from afar
its eyes unblinking

        Camp Red team leader
        hostile environment
        wind masks looming beasts

                craft breaks atmosphere
                BANG! smashes into billboard
                welcome to Target

alien jellyfish
highly venomous tendrils
a lethal game of tag

    a newcomer plants flag
    unknowingly grants
    species citizenship

        blind man, seeing dog
        abductors debate on room
        which one to release?

craft lands on bayou
gators approach — large numbers
mistaken natives

humans land on Mars
aliens offer slice of cake
took you long enough

astrophysics class
bored Martian, fidgets and draws
humans on notebook

soda factory pit stop
worst case scenario
alien on sugar rush

new parameters
for AI intelligent life
pass in your papers

astronauts in cave
marvel at paintings on wall
creatures in space suits

captain's last transmission
that's what they want
cancel rescue party

          galactic auction
          crude communication device
          mobile phone from Earth

                    baby slimes diaper
                    this human is defective
                    Martian sniffs the air

contraption of torture
scare off would-be invaders
gym treadmill in motion

Mercurian moves to Earth
sends message back home:
FREEZING MY ANTENNAE!

Martian toilet talk
when yellow, let it mellow
if brown, check for slugs

pseudo-eclipse
alien battle cruiser
blocks afternoon sun

polar ice caps melt
rising temperature takes toll
ancient aircraft found

cloaking device active
unseen creature approaches
unsuspecting hikers

museum painting
staggering discovery
UFO brush stroke

       alien prank... VOTE!
       runs for presidential seat
       an orange-haired clone

              record storm, blew in
              SMASH! Mile-high tidal wave
              surfer's paradise

first Earthling encounter
peaceful gesture
met with pitchforks and clubs

Elvis is dead?... nope
crank up the teleporter
time the king phones home

couple takes selfie
alien smiles for pic... "CHEESE!"
trolls screams, "PHOTOSHOP!"

baffling broadcast
satellite signal lost
I DEMAND BAYWATCH

    feral creatures converge
    astronaut listens to jazz
    everyone's a critic

        alien botanist
        says, "exotic specimen"
        Earthlings call it a weed

infected team member
standard protocol
companion pulls trigger

aerial dogfight
NOTE: foes do not need propellers
squadron turns back

broken canister
parasitic organism
out in the open

sedated alien wakes
enter pass code
can't remember last digit

eight inch-thick steel doors
automatic with full clip
still no guarantee

Martian steps on Lego
blame Lucy's kid Josh
for the end of the world

interrogation
confiscated contraband
breath mints and death ray

newly discovered planet
ninety percent ocean
scaly inhabitants roam

anti-gravity chamber
throw up or throw down
upset stomach may occur

well, in other news…
an opera singer summons
love-starved alien

    mother calls out to child
    hands over jacket
    cool ninety below outside

        beauty pageant scandal
        aliens nab Miss Universe
        demanding queen's ransom

flash of lightning
thunderclouds perfect cover
spacecraft descends

      green cornfield circles
      Martian patience poked at
      Scarecrow remains still

           ship door slides open
           galactic ambassador
           bows to tumbleweeds

trapped those fugitive
authorities surround ship
Neptune license plates

planet ruled by birds
disguised humans weigh options
sitting ducks... QUACK, QUACK!

bestowed on humans
the secret to time travel
guidelines in Martian

cosplay convention
alien with no disguise
judged best in costume

much-needed vacation
emerald waters
purple dandelions

locked the alien
in the greenhouse; pollen high
deathly allergies

inside creature's belly
barely alive
acid eating through suit

last of its species
arrival on new planet
must find ideal mate

distress message sent
hunting unnecessary
food is on its way

fresh coffee in cup
alien's weary hands hold
waking hypnic jerk

civilization
aliens hidden beneath
sand? Rover moves on

grocery shopping
aisle seven
seeds of destruction

planning honeymoon
a newly engaged couple
Earth is so passé

Body Snatchers Place
home for the aged alien
clothes all wrinkly

epic tale of success
turns instant celebrity
street artist tags spaceship

invaders mimic natives
probes café and orders
crepes and smoothies. Pinkies Up!

    pilot grunts loudly,
    "All these cornfields look the same"
    lost in Iowa

        tethered to space outpost
        engineer repairs panel
        cord slowly unravels

completion of ship
farewell to those left behind
in time for doomsday

long trek to base
through planet's perilous desert
watch where you step

survivor stumbles
towering cliffs on both sides
inhuman shrieks loud

delicate autopsy
unfamiliar anatomy
blood burning like acid

a quarantine breech
officer hits the button
commences clean slate

elderly alien
gives advice to son
don't take gifts from earthlings

signed upcoming waiver
weekend fieldtrip
oxygen tanks all packed

six-month-long voyage
an inventory error
Whoa, Tabasco sauce!

tracking alien
through jungle—abruptly stops
branches crack above

primitive inhabitants
non-telepathic
will return in fifty years

Martian activist
raises sign high in protest
All Earth lives matter

city dump site
feral dog growls at figure
not of this Earth

writing our names in the sand
vessel beyond salvage
memoirs make poor company

shipwrecked team leader
discovers footprints in sand
moving in circles

self-destruct sequence
taunting cursor blinks promptly
awaiting password

hunter's trophy display room
five-horned winged rhino
and fat-bellied congressman

unfair advantage
intergalactic basketball
winged alien team

savage predator
mimic human voices
don't trust cries for help

eating third cheeseburger
no weight problem here
in zero gravity

charging grizzly bear
aliens retreat to ship
Earthlings are psycho

polar ice caps
reminds visitor of home
frozen landscape

infamous family pic
great granduncle Harry
was human, not alien

touchdown on surface
wave tentacles and say hi
first impressions last

Martian flatulence
noxious odor
opens a portal

opposite reactions
dying sun, light years away
backyard sunflowers bloom

no parkas or sleds
Mercury calendar
summer all year round

monitors turned off
motion sensors triggered... see?
it's coming for us

casualty reports
numbering in the thousands
no signs of dead beast

bovine invaders
leaving desolate planet
to greener pastures

first visit to Earth
alien race from Pluto
instant skin cancer

blinding light outside
Uncle Jim picks up shotgun
do not go out there

angry homemaker
spaceship lands in his backyard
week's laundry ruined

craft zips past Andromeda
wife nags pilot
should have asked for directions

toddler picks up object
swallows shiny disc
rest in peace young, Ztirf

intentions unknown
diplomats greet visitors
snipers on standby

stranded alien
unable to contact home
such poor reception

Martian demands a cup of joe
caffeine psychosis
 incinerated barista

Comedian jokes
alien spectator yawns
draws laser blaster

alien garbage dump
stone formations
of unknown origin

clutching bleeding wound
only human remaining
Dammit... Trust No One

meteor shower
distraction for an assault
lovely streaks in sky

tentacle on weapon
heated debate
spectators back away

crawling into war
an alien race of bugs
smeared under our shoes

botched visit to Earth
ship lands in the Atlantic
creates tsunami

smog and filthy waters
tears blind human
Earth is over... again

rusting metal skeletons
alien documents
the remains of skyscraper

nuclear silos open
pilot struggles with map
rockets locked onto spaceship

alien device
unable to stop countdown
PEACE... nice knowin' ya!

harness tears
spinning towards black hole
well, this sucks

yanking safety cord
emergency procedure
with its tentacle

alien take selfies
photos for posterity
beside porta-potties

computer voice speaks,
"select 1 to fire cannon
press 2 for Abba"

collect call from Mars
do you accept the charges?
phone line goes dead... how rude

Hey Future Flyers!
you drive like Aunt Znorb
at the speed of light

travel advisory
avoid blue planet
only one star review

surfing competition
medical nightmare
surfboards melt in magma

Martian class field trip
Look! — ancient Earth artefact
Starbucks paper cup

weekend camping trip
rustle in the bushes
oh you, darn humans

pilot ejects from craft
avoids a fiery crash
but splats against billboard

This experiment
is brought to you by…I mean
we know… 575

About the Haiku Scientist

Aurelio Rico Lopez III is a fan of all things weird and spooky. He is the author of various fiction and poetry books, including: *A Predisposition for Madness, Not the Forgiving Kind, When the Lights Go Out, Far Out, Kaiju Double Barrel, and Easier Dead Than Done.* Aurelio enjoys music, reading, daydreaming, and COFFEE. He hails from Iloilo City, Philippines.

Other Book from

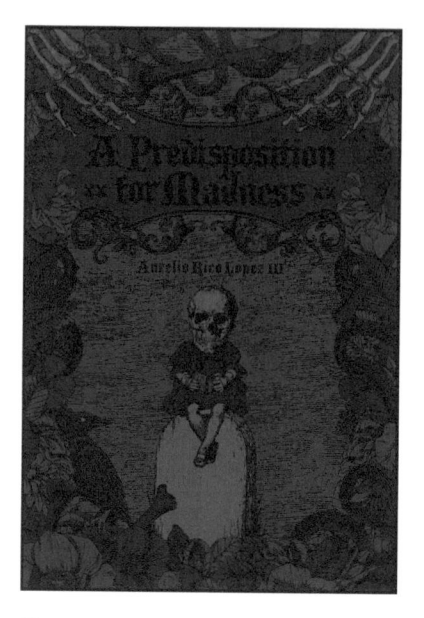

The indication of suffering with madness under peculiar situations; dire consequences and a baggage of other genre bending horror verse with a propensity of violence. This substantial collection depicts a deathly theme that arrays in no particular order and inks madness in all its forms. Aurelio's lunacy is sometimes gruesome, haunting, or cadaverous—the tendency that something is likely to happen is heavy and leaves no burdens behind.

Ferrante calls upon the crickets from all parts of the field. Bringing together distant oceans, mysteries under neighboring moons, love intentions and declarations with a poetic spell. Her imagery speaks with sips of absinthe, touching the orb of the night and returning to familiar, capricious circles of splendor. A terminology the poet calls, "wondertale" you can see for yourself the magic it delivers from her mindful inception and its continuous choir that sings long after.

Hybrid Sequence Media

Ruffle those feathers ladies and gents, these anti-poetry mash-ups throw eggs like curveballs, with no rhyme or reason. THE CHICKENS DON'T CARE... THIS IS THE GREATEST BOOK EVER! Ninja chickens munching on birdseed of eternal damnation, toting machine guns, and sometimes kicking us where it hurts. After everything flies out the coop, you're growing desire of lust for chickens will all begin to make sense.

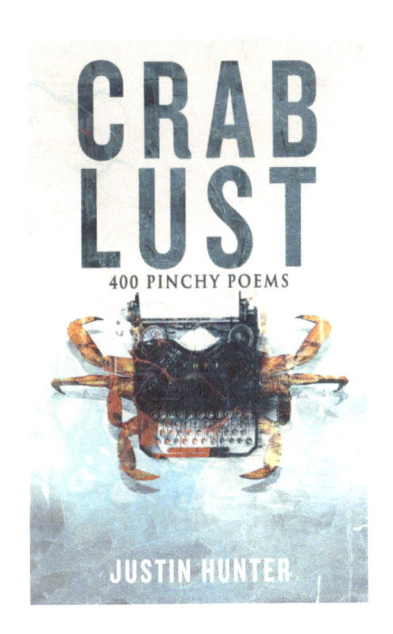

Hunter returns to the LUST series after ruffling our feathers with all of them chickens. Now the CRABS are pinching. These hard-shell anti-poetry romps flips the sandcastles upside down and takes you not just to the beach, but into the mind of these collective crustaceans. With 400 poems about crabs, you could say Mr. Hunter is an omniscient on these exoskeleton critters.